SCHOLASTIC Phonics

Do You Like Music?

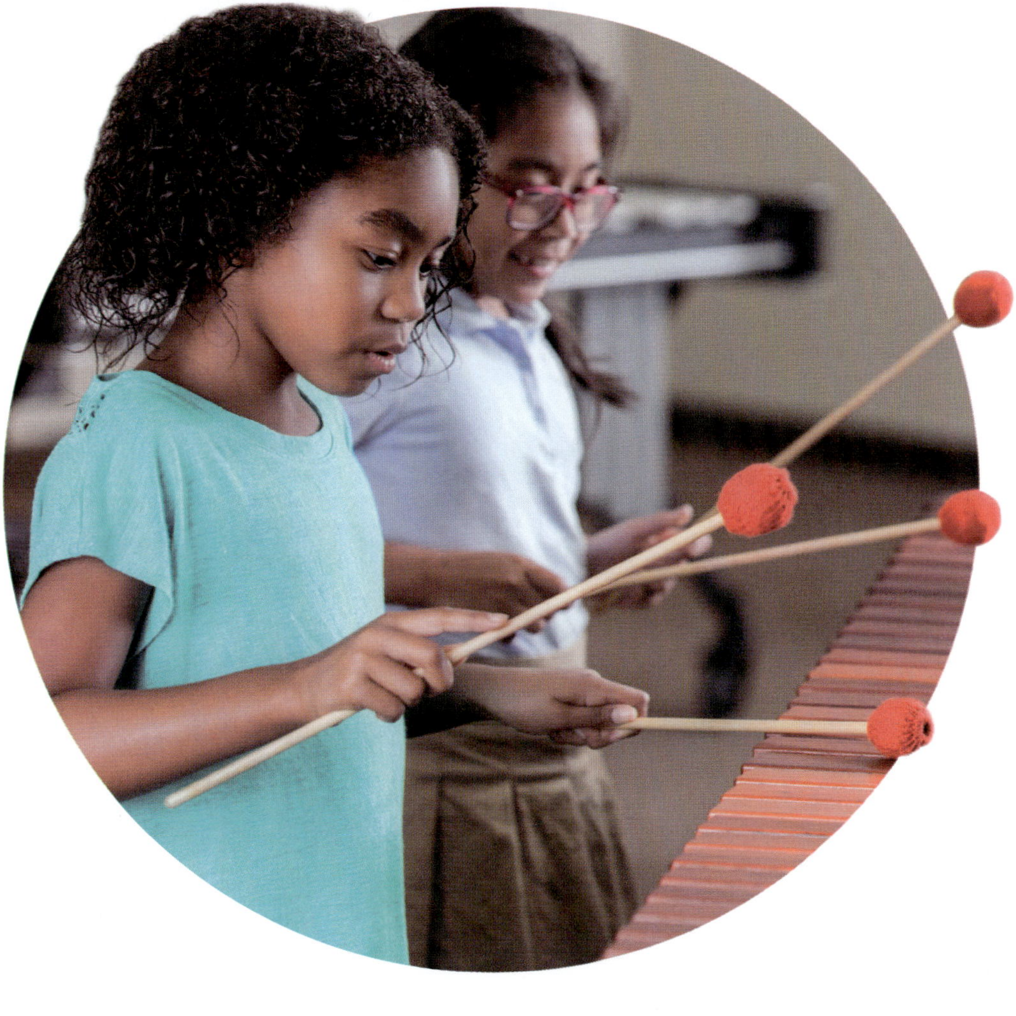

Published in the UK by Scholastic Education, 2023
Scholastic Distribution Centre, Bosworth Avenue, Tournament Fields, Warwick, CV34 6UQ
Scholastic Ireland, 89E Lagan Road, Dublin Industrial Estate, Glasnevin, Dublin, D11 HP5F

SCHOLASTIC and associated logos are trademarks and/or registered trademarks of Scholastic Inc.
www.scholastic.co.uk
© 2023 Scholastic
1 2 3 4 5 6 7 8 9   3 4 5 6 7 8 9 0 1 2

Printed by Ashford Colour Press
The book is made of materials from well-managed, FSC®-certified forests and other controlled sources.

A CIP catalogue record for this book is available from the British Library.
ISBN 978-0702-32106-1

All rights reserved. This book is sold subject to the condition that it shall not, by way of trade or otherwise, be lent, hired out or otherwise circulated in any form of binding or cover other than that in which it is published. No part of this publication may be reproduced, stored in a retrieval system, or transmitted in any form or by any other means (electronic, mechanical, photocopying, recording or otherwise) without prior written permission of Scholastic.

Every effort has been made to trace copyright holders for the works reproduced in this publication, and the publishers apologise for any inadvertent omissions.

Author
Suzy Ditchburn
Editorial team
Rachel Morgan, Vicki Yates, Caroline Hale, Jennie Clifford
Design team
Dipa Mistry, Andrea Lewis, We Are Grace
Photographs
Cover HRAUN/iStock
p5, 11 (classic violin) by_nicholas/iStock
p5 (drums) pepifoto/iStock
p4 (flute) pixhook/iStock
p4 (bagpipes) blindtoy99/iStock
p5 (clarinet) Nikand4/iStock
p4 (trombone) adventtr/iStock
p6 antoniodiaz/Shutterstock
p7 (madolin) syolacan/iStock
p7 (banjo) Image Source Trading Ltd/Shutterstock
p8–9 Angelafoto/Shutterstock
p10, 24 recep-bg/iStock
p3, 11 (electric violin) Svitlana Varfolomieieva/iStock
p12, 24 (piccolo) vandervelden/iStock
p12 (flute) Wavebreakmedia/iStock
p13 (trombone) wernerimages/iStock
p13 (recorder) katleho Seisa/iStock
p14 (clarinet) AleksandarGeorgiev/iStock
p14 (reed) coopder1/iStock
p15 SusanHSmith/iStock
p16 FatCamera/iStock
p17 Gannet77/iStock
p1, 18 SDI Productions/iStock
p19 Churairat Music/iStock
p20 Mr Twister/Shutterstock
p21 Onradio/iStock
p22 Highwaystarz-Photography/iStock
p23, 24 sturti/iStock

Help your child to read!

This book practises these letters and letter sounds.
Point and say the sounds with your child:

- o (as in 'violin')
- i (as in 'kinds')
- e (as in 'be')
- a–e (as in 'name')
- i–e (as in 'like')
- u–e (as in 'tune')
- e–e (as in 'these')

Your child may need help to read these common tricky words:

- what
- of
- do
- you
- when
- the
- have
- some
- to
- are
- one
- could

Before reading
- Look at the cover picture and read the title together. Read the back cover blurb to your child.
- Ask your child: *Do you know the names of any musical instruments?*
- Talk about the image in the magnifying glass.

During reading
- If your child gets stuck on a word, remind them to sound it out and then blend the sounds to read the word: v-i-o-l-i-n, violin.
- If they are still stuck, show them how to read the word.
- Enjoy looking at the pictures together. Pause to talk about the information.

After reading
- Talk about the images on page 24. What can your child tell you about them?
- Ask your child: *What makes the sound louder in string instruments?*
- Discuss with your child which instrument they would like to play. Ask them to explain why they have chosen this instrument.

What kinds of music do you like?

Can you play a tune on an instrument?
Do you like singing?

Can you name these instruments?

String instruments create a sound from strings running along it. When you pluck or rub the strings, a sound is made as the strings vibrate.

violin

mandolin

banjo

Most string instruments have these parts.

neck

hole

strings

tuning pegs

Some have a hole to make the sound louder.

Some string instruments are electric. The sound is louder.

electric bass

The electric violin and classic violin are related.

Wind instruments are shaped like a tube.

piccolo

flute

trombone

recorder

The air vibrates in the tube to make a sound.

Some wind instruments use a reed to make a sound.

clarinet

reed

These bagpipes use a set of bags and tubes to make a sound.

If you don't like the sound of wind instruments, you might prefer one of these instruments.

bongo drum

You can use hands or sticks to make music.

steel pan drum

This instrument is made up of wooden bars. You hit the wooden bars with mallets.

The pipes underneath make the sound louder.

This bass drum makes the deepest sound.

Most pop bands use a bass drum to keep the beat.

If you cannot find an instrument you like, you might prefer to sing.

You could be a solo singer or you could sing in a band.

Talk about it!